The Road to Ballybunion

A Magical Journey Through the Golf and Lore of Southwest IRELAND

JOHN DEGARMO / PAINTINGS BY RAY ELLIS

LONGSTREET PRESS, INC.
Atlanta, Georgia

Published by LONGSTREET PRESS, INC.
a subsidiary of Cox Newspapers,
a subsidiary of Cox Enterprises, Inc.
2140 Newmarket Parkway
Suite 122
Marietta, Georgia 30067

Printed in the United States of America
1st printing, 1997

Library of Congress Catalog Number 97-71941

ISBN: 1-56352-433-3

Ektachromes of paintings by Michael Kraft
Jacket and book design by Jill Dible

The Road to
Ballybunion

Ireland

It's still a place of castles
And thatched-roof cottages.
A land of music and easy laughter.
In Ireland, we often find ourselves
Quite behind the times.
And in no particular hurry to catch up.

(Except on our golf.)

Along the Road

Sunday on The Ring

Introduction

The road to Ballybunion may take many shapes and forms.

It may be an actual road — a narrow sliver of macadam clinging to the sides of rocky Irish cliffs where unfenced sheep graze. More than half-a-dozen such roads lead to the sleepy village of Ballybunion, perched on the edge of the Shannon Estuary in Southwest Ireland.

It may be an alluring photograph in a glossy travel brochure, designed to excite your imagination and make you phone your travel agent before dinner. You've seen the photo — a gauzy image of golfers walking a narrow path between towering, grassy dunes in pursuit of their perfect shots launched into a fading rainbow. We've all hit that shot from the safety of our living rooms.

Or the road may be only a long-held dream — an ambitious goal driven by ancestry and a common name — shrouded in mystery like the ruins of ancient Celtic castles that dot the countryside of County Kerry.

But whether you're an international golfer or an armchair traveler, the road to Ballybunion will seduce you with its physical beauty, its history, its quiet charm, and the promise of a once-in-a-lifetime golfing experience. It is that rare treat that turns out to be every bit as tasty as you imagined.

Our journey began like so many others — in conversation over a cool drink following a round of golf. After replaying the highlights of the most recent round, our talk turned to Scotland, the birthplace of golf. We had each been there and been mesmerized by the stunning natural beauty of the seaside courses, called "links" by some golfers because of the way the holes are linked together like a chain along a craggy coastline. We swapped stories of colorful caddies, of peculiar holes, of treacherous weather conditions that strangely added to the enjoyment of the round, and then we fell awkwardly silent as the longing inside us grew.

"As wonderful as Scotland is," said one of our group, filling the dead air, "Ireland is even better."

Better? Better than Royal Dornoch, better than Gullane, better than Carnoustie and the hallowed St. Andrews?

"There are still great but relatively unknown courses in Ireland. The landscapes rival anything anywhere in the world. The people are charming, it's not too expensive, and it's easy to get around. And, of course, there's Ballybunion, my favorite golf course in the world."

Three voices responded almost in unison, "When do we leave?"

That was the first step on our road to Ballybunion. Four months later we were in a car, driving on the "wrong" side of the road, leaving Shannon Airport to explore golf in the southwest of Ireland. We considered the north, site of the much ballyhooed Royal Portrush and Royal County Down; and we considered the east, where Portmarnock and Royal Dublin rule. But we finally settled on the southwest in general, and County Kerry in particular, because of its abundance of interesting courses … and because the road led to Ballybunion, the jewel in Ireland's golfing crown.

— *Chuck Perry, Editor*

Bucolic. *The pastoral-historical ambience as you wind through the roads of Kerry is more than merely interesting…it's almost inspirational.*

Prologue

GETTING PROPERLY "IRISHED"

In the early 1960s, while trying to establish myself and my company as the answer to many advertisers' needs, I heard from a friend in the publishing business that the Irish Tourist Board — Bord Fáilte — wasn't very happy with the country's tourism growth. In fact, Ireland's growth was anemic relative to the burgeoning European tourist trade.

As CEO of an advertising agency, itself trying to "burgeon," it was my job to get new business … to convince marketers that we could help them build their business better than the other guy. Looking back, I realize that we had far more enthusiasm than credentials. But I did have the good sense to have married a woman named Murphy, and that fact was not wasted on my Irish prospects.

Our pitch to the Irish Tourist Board was quite simple: To grow its tourism satisfactorily, Ireland needed more people with names like deGarmo or Luppanacci or Jankowski, who traveled about the countryside and fished and played golf and frequented the nice hotels and restaurants and shops, as opposed to only Kellys and Ryans and O'Neills, who had come to Ireland only to bunk in with and rekindle relationships with a previous generation.

Two weeks after our presentation, on a rainy Friday afternoon at about 4:45, my phone rang and Bord Fáilte General Manager Kevin Durnin said, "John, I think I have some news for you that's not all bad." This reluctant, typically Irish message was a precursor for our association over the next three years, during which time we didn't get near to Ireland. The Tourist Board seemed almost embarrassed about its country and directed us to follow a very low-key approach to its advertising campaigns.

We were positive that we could do a better job for them by following our own strategy, so finally I said to Kevin, "The only way we can effectively do what we're being paid to do is to go to Ireland and find out for ourselves what we're promoting. Let us drive through your country, fish in your streams, challenge your golf courses, shop your shops, and talk to your people. If we don't end up with a better advertising strategy and program, we'll pay for the trip. If we do, you'll pay for it."

We went, we saw, we fell in love, we returned, we convinced; and thus the direction of advertising for Ireland changed dramatically, as did the results. Today, through the effort of many more since our 1960s foray, Ireland is one of the fastest growing tourist sites in the world.

I often get the feeling that many non-Irish people want to adopt the "Emerald Isle" as their own. How many times have you seen a group on March 17th going a cappella with "Danny Boy" or "Macushla," as if the songs were their personal anthem?

One might suspect that this passion grows from the charm of Irish people, and of course it does. But the charm also emanates from the countryside and the unique manner of speech the people use. Although most Irish people speak English, Gaelic is the true national language, and the colorful history of that language accounts for much of the uniqueness of expression.

Once, while motoring in the back country, I stopped to ask a pedestrian for directions. Instead of telling me to go straight, he said, "Don't make a turn."

On another drive, I stopped for gas and nature's call. When I asked the proprietor the location of the men's room, he pointed to the edge of the tarmac on which his gas station stood and said, "Anywhere between there and Dublin."

And then there's that legendary Irish charm, candor, and grace. Once in a small, local bar in Dublin, I got into a conversation with a patron. He asked what I was doing there from America, and I explained I was observing Irish lifestyles for an advertising campaign in the American market. He took a drink of his stout and said, "This bar is a bad example tonight. Normally there'd be a fight by now. Would you like me to start one?"

Finally, you'll feel an almost "so be it" attitude among the Irish which underlines their delightful dispositions. And, there is a private side too: You'll not be able to saunter to any bar, sit on a stool, order a beer and get into the immediate conversations you might in many other "watering holes" around the world. No, you'll have to ease into the conversation with your nearby stool-mate…and once you have, and then depart the pub for your saunter back to your digs, you'll feel you've made a friend. And, well you might have!

MEMORABLE GAME

The American golfer drove his car into the parking lot of one of Ireland's more formidable courses. He was anxious to better his round of a year ago. As he pulled his bag from his trunk, he noticed his caddie from the previous year approaching the car. He greeted the caddie enthusiastically and asked, "Do you remember me from last year?"

"Oh, yes sir," said the caddie. "And has your game improved?"

Irish Attitudes

Before "teeing it up" about several of Ireland's great golf courses and their surroundings, it seems logical to "warm up" about Ireland itself, for the country, the courses, and the towns they're in or near are intimately bound to each other.

The game of golf is full of paradoxes: Aim left to go right; aim right to hit left; swing easy to hit hard; hit down to make the ball go up; etc. Ireland also is a paradox of sorts. There she sits jutting out into the North Atlantic. To her east is England, her conqueror and neighbor. To her west is the desolate ocean in which the fingers of Clogher Head, Castletownbere, and Waterville seem poised to stroke their way the two thousand miles or so to America.

Nearly seven hundred miles to her north sits the slightly larger island of Iceland. Legend has whispered that Ireland was populated when a boatload of

Heading towards The Ring

Norsemen, headed for Iceland, were shipwrecked on their way. Iceland is perceived to be cold and distant; yet smaller Ireland is perceived as warm and welcoming. The Gulf Stream meanders from the southwest Atlantic, between the Americas, to soothe Ireland with its warm breezes dramatically enough to allow palm trees to flourish in Dublin.

And the paradox continues; take St. Patrick's Day in America, for example. While it's just another day in Ireland, albeit a holy day, the streets of New York are filled with paraders waving shamrocks and wielding shillelaghs, kids in kilts, and men in emerald-colored trousers with matching plastic hats. The colloquial "Top o' the morning," an expression totally unknown in Ireland, gushes from the lips of all nationalities and colors, and it ends up being part of the commitment to being slightly Irish … "great, great, great aunt on my mother's side."

This perception of a happy, wondrous nation must be tempered with its serious accomplishments, too.

The conquest of Ireland in the twelfth century by the English resulted in the stifling of Irishmen's ability to express themselves in their own language; the use of Gaelic in any form was outlawed. Yet Gaelic is a mandatory part of today's educational system, and the Irish are a naturally loquacious and articulate nation. The Irish, in fact, have been said to out-English the

Overlooking Lough Leane

English with their gift for language.

The Irish have given the world, besides the safety pin, great scholars; mythology surpassed perhaps only by the Greeks; mysterious castles; interesting forms of music and dance, such as the immensely popular Riverdance; many poets and writers such as William Butler Yeats and James Joyce; playwrights George Bernard Shaw and Oscar Wilde; and old attitudes and convictions that lend perspective to life in the new world.

And, the Irish have given us golf, too; not alone, but enough so that despite the numerous and marvelous courses in Scotland, true golfers have been known to nod agreeably to the comment, "The best courses in Scotland are in Ireland."

More than just playing golf, however, the Irish have romanced the game with an admirable manner and

Vintage Links

philosophy: Whereas most Americans play golf to win, most Irish play it to enjoy it.

This difference in attitudes was demonstrated during a recent golfing trip to Ireland. Playing a 420-yard par four into the teeth of a prevailing Irish wind, one member of our foursome hit a great drive and a career three-wood, only to find himself still forty yards short of the green. "This hole is unfair in these conditions," he groused to his caddie. "There's no way to get on in two."

With the glint of wisdom in his eye, the caddie answered, "Beg pardon, Sir, but the par on this hole is four, and you've struck only two shots." As the truth of this statement sunk into our embarrassed playing partner, the caddie added, "The notion of 'on in two and two

putts for par' is an American invention; we prefer to think of such holes merely as par fours."

But par can be a very elusive score when the Irish wind is up and a steady mist is blowing horizontally, or when an errant shot is held captive by unforgiving rough. Under such conditions, it is not unusual to make double- or triple-bogeys, or even worse.

Consequently, many Irish golfers prefer match play to medal (or stroke) competition. Making an eight on one hole of match play means you probably lost the hole but are still in the match, whereas making an eight in medal play means you're probably done for the day. Which way would you say is most enjoyable?

Chalk up another one for the Irish.

Q & A

We were headed down the fairway of No. 11 at Waterville, a difficult and extremely tight par five. With our tee shots safely in the fairway, our second shots left us a blind approach to a green nestled among mounds of long grass. It was clearly too dangerous to try to get home in two, so placement of the blind second shot was essential for a chance at par.

Perhaps in an effort to gain a modicum of confidence before hitting this testy shot, our golfing partner that day asked his caddie, "What's on either side of the fairway down in the landing area?"

Showing the depths of his wisdom and humor, the caddie answered politely but firmly, "Rough, sir."

DAYS OF YORE

uthor Robert T. Sommers tells a story worth repeating in his enjoyable book *Golf Anecdotes.*

The great Irish amateur Joe Carr was playing a casual round at Rosses Point in County Sligo in western Ireland, the site of many triumphant performances earlier in his career. From 1953-67, Carr had won three British Amateurs, six Irish Amateurs, had played in ten Walker Cup competitions, and had captained the 1965 team. He was arguably the best amateur golfer ever to come out of Ireland.

Well past his best days of competitive golf but still enjoying the game, Joe was having a bad day at Rosses Point. He sent shots left and right, seldom hit a green, and putted poorly.

His young caddie not only did not know him but had never heard of him. Trying to ease Carr's growing agitation, the caddie asked, "Have you played Rosses Point before, sir?"

"Oh, yes," Joe answered. "Many times."

"You know they play the West of Ireland championship here, sir," the caddie went on.

"Yes, I know," said Joe. "I won it twelve times."

The caddie thought for a moment and then offered, "It must have been fierce easy to win in those days, sir."

Nature's Way. *If St. Andrews has its Hell Bunker, what might you call this Irish Monster? As varied and venomous as Irish course bunkers appear…they all seem so natural as they follow the flow of the land.*

Megalith

During their three and a half centuries of rule in Ireland, the Norse made an
indelible impression on the Emerald Isle. Today, ruins and several rich archeological
sites stand in evidence of the Vikings' long sojourn in the land. Excavations at many
of the sites have yielded houses, swords, jewelry, and ships from that era.
This one sits just moments from the town of Ballybunion.

Why County Kerry?

County Kerry, the focal point of this book, is a particularly gentle place — especially its people. The ones who work in restaurants and pubs, the people you meet at golf courses or marinas, even the residents who nod as you walk the streets or yield as you drive the roads (How can they tell we're Americans?) are all gracious and generous.

But theirs is not a "tourist trap" hospitality. Instead, you can almost feel a "so be it" attitude among the people, an attitude that fosters acceptance and depth. No one may yell out a welcome or jump up to shake your hand when you enter a pub, but you'll soon find yourself involved in a hearty conversation with the local publicans, and before you know it you'll have made a friend for life.

The gently plunging Ring coastline

Kerry is very historic. Tralee was there in 1603. Dingle, too. And only a dozen years later Ardfert was established. Ballybunion? Records indicate that the remains of the castle you see there today were already ruins in 1580.

The remoteness and simplicity of Kerry were evident as recently as 1980, when there was no telephone service available after 2 p.m. on Sundays. If you wanted to make a call, you'd have to hop in your car and drive forty or fifty miles to the next county. That is, if you had a car!

Bucolic as the land may be, Ireland and County Kerry have progressed in many ways in recent years, partly to accommodate the growing throngs of tourists. Many are surprised to learn that sitting quietly in a small Kerry village is an office of New York Life Insurance Company, processing claims for the United

Grazing near Dingle Bay

States' customer. Beyond Kerry, in Galway, an Irish hour or two north, is a McGraw-Hill office handling worldwide magazine renewals.

Other American companies have computer linkups with offices in Kerry and elsewhere that permit processing administrative functions at lower costs of highly trained personnel. This work in many cases is done while America sleeps and then is "on your desk" when you get there in the morning.

When you talk with managers of Irish business and industry, they're aware of their laid-back image of years ago, but they remind us that there are many different ways to motivate people. As one pointed out, the shortest distance between two points for a German manager might be a straight line, but for an Irish manager the shortest distance may be a zigzag.

∞∞∞

The daily pace is a good deal slower here than in the States. That fact was reinforced time and again as we traveled around County Kerry in search of interesting golf courses and Irish cheer. Although road signs were plentiful, we often found them to be confusing or even contradictory. We would stop to ask distance and direction, and invariably the advice we received would be wrong.

"How far to Dooks golf course?" we might ask.

"Oh, I'd say another ten kilometers on your left. Shouldn't take more than a few minutes," would come the obliging answer. Half an hour later, we would still be driving the speed limit in search of Dooks, which turned out to be 35 kilometers away.

When we quizzed one of the locals about these common errors of time and distance, he looked a bit puzzled and then answered, "If you've made up your mind to go to Dooks, what does it matter how far it is or how long it takes? You'll be there when you get there."

We came to refer to these instances as "Irish minutes" and "Irish miles," which meant pay no attention to estimates of time or distance and try instead to enjoy the journey. You'll be there when you get there.

∞∞∞

The Gaels came to Ireland just before Christ. They must have done something right, because they're still there, and I haven't met a soul who isn't glad.

Comment from an Irish father whose two sons had been asked to leave the golf course for poor conduct:

"'Tis a poor family that cannot afford one gentleman!"

The Road to Ballybunion

Like most people who visit Ireland for the first time, I was overwhelmed by the Irish people — their politeness, their generosity of spirit, their simple and sincere kindness. But it was many days after my arrival that I discovered one of the sources of their warm and open Irish hearts, and I found it, quite literally, on "the road to Ballybunion."

On our recent two-week trip, our intrepid foursome covered nearly seven hundred miles of twisting, turning, tight, sometimes harrowing little roads getting to and from our Irish golfing destinations. Unlike American roads, where every town is signified by an exit sign on the highway, in Ireland there are no real "highways" as we know them. To get from Dingle to Ballybunion, or from Cahirsiveen to Tralee, or from Killarney to Waterville, you have no choice except to drive right through the heart of each and every town between the two. No bypass, no highway, no clever way to speed up the trip by skirting these beautiful little towns.

In the pedal-to-the-metal consciousness of most American drivers, myself included, this was a very frustrating way to travel…if you could even call it travel.

No real highway…

Meandering would be a more appropriate description. But after a few days of such meandering, a funny thing happened: I found that I didn't mind those little delays so much. In fact, I actually began to look forward to each and every little enclave.

It occurred to me one morning, as I waited patiently for a farmer and his cows to cross the road, that one secret to the charm and generosity of the Irish people just might be found in those Irish roads.

When you travel from town to town, as the Irish people do themselves and as we were doing, you see the faces of the residents of each village; you stop for children at the crosswalks and see the fields where they play; you witness shopkeepers open, close, or tend their stores; you see churches where townspeople get married and pray; you see cemeteries where they've buried their dead for hundreds of years. After seeing all this — town after town, day after day — I began to understand that perhaps the generous and caring spirit that the Irish people exude is rooted in the way they are all connected to each other — in the roads.

Those lovely Irish roads connect their lives, and in subtle but profound ways, they make all of Ireland a community in the truest sense. Ireland is a place where your neighbor becomes like family, and where a group of golfers becomes richer for having experienced it.

— *Matthew deGarmo*

Cap of the Road

THE WEATHER

And finally, before hitting the road to Ballybunion, there's the inescapable issue of the weather in Ireland. Many people think of Ireland and inclement weather as almost a single entity — you can't have one without the other.

Years ago my ad agency created an advertisement for the Irish Tourist Board. Its headline read:

Sure, we get a lot of rain in Ireland.

Measured by inches, we get almost as much as Miami.

That's a fact, and the ad worked beautifully, yet many people remain suspicious of the fast- and ever-changing Irish weather. My advice is to enjoy it. I'd rather be rained on in Ireland than shined on in most of the rest of the world.

Writer Michael MacLiammoir expressed a similar attitude, although certainly more poetically, in a 1966 book. He said, "Ireland, you see, is full of the strangest contradictions, and in this indeed she is not unique, although it would seem that nowhere else, in Europe, at any rate, are there such extremes of desolation and brilliance, poverty and

riches, apathy and energy, idiocy and intellect, blindness and vision, wanton callousness and imaginative sympathy, mental fog and cerebral clarity. The weather repeats the fickle uncertainty of these humors; there is no answer can be found to the stranger's question, 'What is the best time of the year to visit your country?'"

It may be a warm, golden morning in November or February, or a chilly one in June. But no matter what the weather, your enduring impression of Ireland will be the people, for they are the country's greatest bounty.

Weather or not

It was a five-hour round that included numerous excursions after lost balls, untold delays to get closer views of this cliff or that beach, too many photographs, and all this combined with a mediocre golf game that produced scores in the low 100s. At the merciful end of it all, one member of the foursome turned to his caddie and asked,

"What do I owe you?"

To which the caddie replied, "An apology."

"Their" Courses and "Ours"

I've often tried to explain the inordinate appeal of links-type courses in Ireland (and yes, in Scotland and England, too). Is it that they look different because they seem to have more moguls and fewer trees and deeper bunkers and firmer fairways and inevitably one "unfair" hole?

One day in 1977 I had the distinct good fortune to be invited to lunch with my friend Rene Dentan, then president of Rolex Watch Inc. in the United States, and pro golfer Hubert Green, who had been featured in a Rolex ad. Green had just returned from that nonpareil shootout at Turnberry in 1977 where Tom Watson had beaten Nicklaus for "the Open" title on the last hole. Green finished third … ten shots back!

At a lull in our conversation, straining a bit to keep it going and being somewhat in awe of Green, I asked

Ballybunion

him how he'd compare the courses "over there" with ours in the U.S. Instantly he responded, "I don't."

I've never forgotten Green's answer. The origins of the courses are so different that they defy valid comparison. And that extreme difference may be the source of the appeal of links courses, particularly to Americans. In most cases, the only earth-movers used on the classic golf courses of the U.K. were God and sheep. God designed the courses, and the sheep contributed the bunkers (as shelter from the weather). All man had to do was recognize the site. Later on, some smart Scot mowed sections of grass a little lower than the rest, dug a hole in the ground and put a stick in it, and called himself a golfer.

By contrast, most U.S. courses — especially those built in the last forty years — have been created by moving around massive amounts of dirt with bulldozers, cutting down existing trees and replanting new ones, sculpting greens and fairways, and installing extensive irrigation systems. God still provided the grass, albeit with help from nurserymen.

One of our stops on the road to Ballybunion was the beautiful Killeen course at Killarney, several miles inland. Although golf has been played here since the late 1880s, the meadowland course bears more resemblance to a plush, newer American course than to the rough-hewn links courses along the coast. Because it was so familiar to us, the Killeen experience was not among our favorites. Yet Irish golfers rave about playing

#12, among Tralee's challenges

at Killarney because it is so different from the more common links courses.

The old saw may be true — there are as many golf course architects in the world as there are players!

SWEET SOUNDS

Few sounds are as melodic and thoroughly pleasant to the ear as the name of Irish towns.

Listen to their poesy:

Dingle	Cahirciveen
Abbeyfeale	Skibbereen
Roscommon	Kilkenny
Glengariff	Listowel
Ballycastle	Roscrea
Enniscorthy	Tulla
Castlerea	Crossmolina
Ennistymon	Lisdoonvarna
Courtmacsherry	Mallow
Lismore	Cushenden
Antrim	Tralee

And what could be more beautiful than Ballybunion?

Troubles

What is a Links Course?

The word "links" continues to befuddle many golfers. How often have you heard someone either try to use the term or explain it, only to stumble over themselves like a high-handicapper might on a finesse shot? This frequently occurs immediately following a trip to Ireland or Scotland and is probably intended to establish the player's credibility as an "experienced links golfer."

If you'll pardon the pun, the term covers a lot of ground. Among the more common definitions I've heard are:

1. A course built along an ocean.

2. A course with nine holes out and nine holes in, so that No. 1 and No. 18 are next to the clubhouse, which is usual, but No. 9 and No. 10 are someplace out in the hinterlands.

3. A course on which the playing conditions are influenced by the tides.

4. A course from which you can see an ocean.

None of the above is as specific as the two that follow:

1. A course built on barren land, often having been inhabited by goats and sheep, originally unkempt by human hand. Its foundation is usually sandy with a delicate grass cover, and the terrain has been shaped by wind, rain, and God. (This definition is courtesy of Noel Cronin, Secretary/Manager at Waterville.)

2. A golf course on sandy "links-land" next to the sea, notable for undulating terrain and the absence of trees, with pot bunkers and firm fairways and greens. (From the book *Links of Heaven.*)

Now, combine the two and you get what I believe is the best definition: **A course built on barren but undulating land, shaped by wind, rain, and God, with a foundation of sandy soil and fairly delicate grass cover**.

Note the "delicate grass cover" mentioned above. If you've played links courses, you're probably familiar with the somewhat unkempt look of the fairways, and yet you usually get good lies on them. That's a peculiar characteristic of links land. Today, however, many of the true links courses are blending other strains of grass into their natural "delicate" surface to toughen them so they can better withstand the increased "traffic."

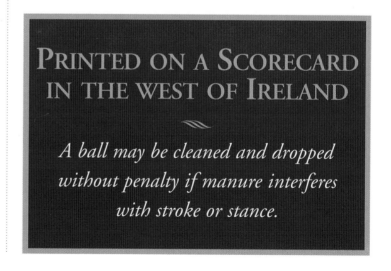

PRINTED ON A SCORECARD IN THE WEST OF IRELAND

A ball may be cleaned and dropped without penalty if manure interferes with stroke or stance.

"Some of the Irish links, I was about to write, stand comparison with the greatest courses in the world. They don't. They are the greatest courses in the world, not only in layout but in scenery and 'atmosphere' and that indefinable something which makes you relive again and again the day you played there."

— HENRY LONGHURST

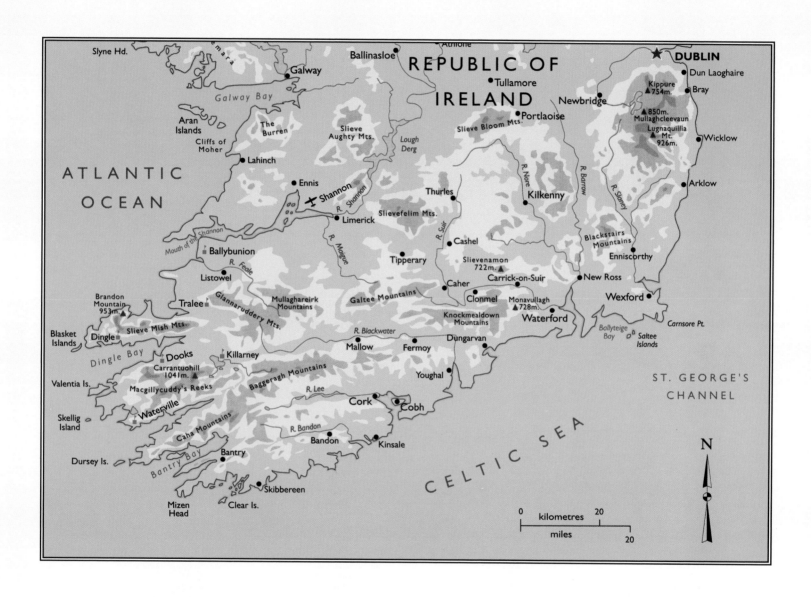

Slyne Hd.

Ballinasloe

REPUBLIC OF
IRELAND

★ **DUBLIN**

Galway

• Tullamore

• Dun Laoghaire

Galway Bay

Kippure
▲754m.

• Bray

Newbridge

The
Burren

Slieve
Aughty Mts.

• Portlaoise

▲850m.
Mullaghcleevaun

Lugnaquillia
Mt.
926m. ▲

• Wicklow

Aran
Islands

*Lough
Derg*

Slieve Bloom Mts.

Cliffs of
Moher

• Lahinch

ATLANTIC

OCEAN

• Ennis

Shannon

Thurles

Kilkenny

• Arklow

R. Nore

R. Barrow

R. Slaney

• Limerick

R. Shannon

Slievefelim Mts.

R. Suir

Blackstairs
Mountains

Mouth of the Shannon

• Cashel

Enniscorthy

Slievenamon
722m. ▲

Ballybunion

R. Feale

Tipperary

R. Maigue

Caher

Carrick-on-Suir

• New Ross

Listowel

Galtee Mountains

Clonmel

• Wexford

Brandon
Mountain
953m. ▲

Tralee

Glannaruddery Mts.

Mullaghareirk
Mountains

Monavullagh
▲728m.

Knockmealdown
Mountains

Carnsore Pt.

Blasket
Islands

Slieve Mish Mts.

R. Blackwater

Dungarvan

Waterford

*Ballyteige
Bay*

Saltee
Islands

Dingle

Dooks

Killarney

Mallow

Fermoy

Dingle Bay

Carrantuohill
1041m. ▲

Youghal

ST. GEORGE'S
CHANNEL

Valentia Is.

Macgillycuddy's Reeks

Baggeragh Mountains

R. Lee

Waterville

Skellig
Island

Caha Mountains

R. Bandon

Cork

Cobh

Dursey Is.

Bantry Bay

Bantry

Bandon

Kinsale

CELTIC SEA

Skibbereen

N

Mizen
Head

Clear Is.

0   kilometres   20

miles

20

25

#12, Tralee

Tralee

Tralee Golf Club sits quietly about 8 miles west of Tralee. Its address is "West Barrow, Ardfert, County Kerry." But take note here. There are a couple of other towns between Tralee and the course, and you may find yourself wondering how so many towns can be in so small an area. Answer: Almost every time a river or stream divides a piece of land here, lo — there's another town. No zip codes, just town after town and mostly without a village. Looking at Tralee Golf Club's address, one might wonder if it's in two towns.

The club itself boasts one of the most stunning seaside courses in the world. As an Arnold Palmer course, it owes its power and beauty both to its natural graces and to those cultivated by its accomplished and daring designer.

#3, Tralee

As the "first Arnold Palmer course in Europe," the present course at Tralee opened to great fanfare in 1984. The reviews for the most part have been rave, and many place Tralee alongside Ballybunion and Waterville as the greatest courses in Southwest Ireland. More obviously designed and constructed than the others, Tralee may not offer the continuity of its peers, but it lacks nothing. The raw beauty of the landscape is so breathtaking it defies description. And the course itself bears the impression of its designer: It is bold, unorthodox, and disarmingly straightforward.

Although the new course opened in 1984, it should be made clear that the tradition of golf in Tralee is long. The Tralee Golf Club was founded in 1896 when 120 interested people paid a subscription price of ten shillings each for membership. After moving to a new location one-quarter mile from the railway station, the club became much more accessible and popular. And to make it more playable, the club stewards hired a manager and paid him the "princely sum of one pound per week." He proved his worth by at least one shrewd arrangement. Instead of charging greens fees the manager purchased seventy sheep which fattened themselves for market by grazing the course. The funds from their sale financed club operations.

In the early 1980s, the members decided that their nine-hole course was too crowded and decided to purchase new land for a full course. That done, they set about hiring the best architect possible. After a bidding war and long meetings filled with negotiations, eating and drinking, they settled on Arnold Palmer and his

#8 green, overlooking Barrow Harbour

associate Ed Seay. (The opportunity to design a course on true linksland is so rare that many designers significantly lowered their bids to get in.) Palmer would direct from the States and Seay would oversee the day-to-day operations on the construction site.

In the end, the partners may have gotten a little more than they bargained for. In defining their course of action, they simply did not account for certain kinds of contingencies. For starters, they did not plan on having

to fly a construction supervisor over from the States because the club could not supply one. Nor did they plan on having the use of only one bulldozer or on having to reseed the windswept course several times. As Americans accustomed to dealing with wealthy developers, they never dreamed of doing without an irrigation system. But the members insisted that the Good Lord would provide the water, and he did. Obviously the Irish do things differently, and, in spite of the hurdles (and perhaps because of them), the team of Seay and Palmer managed to create an incredible golf experience.

Tralee has a plethora of nice people. Eugene O'Callahan, who sees that you get the right caddie and the right start on the course, is truly interested in seeing you enjoy yourself. And Paddy Carey, perhaps the seniormost member, makes sure you do just that, as well as letting you know he has roots in the U.S. — his brother in Cape Cod.

The adventure truly begins at number two, a spell-binding combination of cliff-infused vistas and technical intricacy. To place it in context, let us say that the eighteenth at Pebble Beach borders on mild when compared with the second at Tralee. On the next hole, a Tudor gun turret provides the backdrop for a sensational par three which runs over rocks and is bordered by water.

The triad of the sixth, seventh, and eighth round out the front nine with superb play. The sixth invites you to the right, but you had better be left for at least a chance to get home in two. The multileveled green on seven can tighten up your swing a bit (it plays to about 140

#11, Palmer's Peak where on his first inspection he landed his helicopter

An ampitheatre of dunes surrounds Brocks Hollow, #13

yards). The really wonderful eighth dares you to use your driver. If you do it well, you will have a little pitch and run. And I mean pitch and run — a wedge to the green has little chance of working here.

As for number nine, the best I can say about it is it gets you back to the clubhouse and to number ten.

The back nine is the ultimate. Ten is outstanding because of the second shot — assuming you've hit a fair drive. Eleven, called "Palmer's Peak," offers a let-'er-rip tee shot opportunity. A blind second shot and a boorish green make you work, think, and hope hard. The need for a long putt may even call for a bit of prayer.

I wonder if there are adjectives to describe number twelve. The only expression that comes to mind is "one of the toughest damn holes ever built." Traditional golf, as I have said elsewhere, says a par four should be reached in two and two-putted. Forget it here. Hit a decent drive, and then with anything but a following wind, it's a lay-up. Then a wedge or maybe a nine iron and one putt. If you don't make that, just remember that with a five, you're ahead of most who play the hole.

All the par threes here are great and number thirteen proves no exception. It plays about 150 yards to a slightly intimidating, partially visible green. Compound that with the dunes at the back of the green that seem to billow skyward and your adrenaline will really start pumping.

You'll really get a kick out of fifteen: It is certainly among the top ten in short par fours that I have ever seen. The shot off the tee must carry about 180 yards if you want placement for your second shot. You are better off to the right because then you have a straight shot to the cloistered green.

All you can say about sixteen, poised at cliff's edge, is that it is a terrifying one-shotter at 170 yards from the white. If you're still not terrified, visit the blues for a look, but only a look. You should be scratch caliber or better to play it from there. Seventeen is a short, but no slouch, par four. The audacious fairway runs along the cliffs, first to the left between the dunes, and then to another daunting, dune-lined fairway shot that leaves you a shot to a very

reasonable green. Eighteen is not as scenic as its predecessors, but it should not be too tough. The simple and very nice clubhouse just beyond the green is motivation enough to make it home in two good shots.

As famous as Tralee is for golf, the area offers more than the game. The town serves as the gateway to the Dingle peninsula and prides itself on its many markets, its interesting shops, and its broad range of restaurants. Another source of pride and identity for the area is the annual Rose of Tralee contest. Entrants who are either Irish or of Irish descent come from every county in Ireland and from many areas around the world (Ever heard of the Rose of Chicago or of Singapore?) to compete for the title. The aspiring contestants must qualify through interviews and then demonstrate a talent, such as singing, dancing, poetry, or acting as a mime, etc.. The entire town involves itself in entertaining its guests and providing a good time for all.

If you have ever heard the song "The Rose of Tralee," I will wager it has made you want to see or has made you grateful for having seen the green mountains, blue sea, and the "beautiful vale of Tralee." The rewards are great for anyone (golfer and nongolfer alike) who makes the trip.

#16 from the middle tee

Tributary

From the dunes, the wind, and the sea,
To a kinder, more peaceful site.

Before leaving two of the seaside challenges enjoyed on a recent visit to Ireland, Tralee and Waterville, we asked a handful of people their opinion of Killarney, our next "game." Despite the provincial nature of the Irish universe, each of the four people questioned commented that their local members loved to go to Killarney because it is so different from what they're used to.

No dunes, no wind, no gorse, no cliffs, Killarney is a serene and very beautiful golf location. Overshadowed by Macgillycuddy's Reeks, the highest and most beautiful of Ireland's mountains, Killarney offers two courses: Killeen, the site of the 1991 and 1992 Irish Open, and Mahony's Point.

Although golf was played here as early as the late 1880s, the "joining" of members to Killarney didn't happen until 1893, when forty locals each put up ten

shillings to enjoy the generosity of the first Earl of Kenmare, who gave them the use of Deer Park for a course.

Lord Castlerosse

The course enjoyed increasing popularity but little attention was devoted to development.

In the 1930s, the next Earl of Kenmare, known better as Lord Castlerosse, emerged as the champion of progress for the club. His early life, however, did not indicate much promise. While at university, he spent his money and time on food, women, and idle pleasures. Later he was reduced to writing a gossip column for a London paper to cover his debts. In general, his pursuits failed to reveal any hint of ambition until he was struck by the idea of building a resort and golf course in Killarney.

With the help of local merchants and independent investors, ground was broken in 1937 and work was completed, on schedule, in 1939. Castlerosse had his course, and he happily devoted the remaining years of his life (he died in 1943) to making slight improvements and changes in the design. Because of his untimely death, however, he never saw the implementation of his most colorful idea, planting each hole on the course with a different colored flower, or the realization of his most outrageous concept, setting up a sound system to broadcast Beethoven's Ninth Symphony across the fairways at noontime! It was no matter. The course immediately earned the acclaim of the golfing world and secured Castlerosse's place in the history of the Irish game as the man who successfully circumvented worldwide depression to build the course and improve tourism in the region.

In the 1950s, the course experienced another transformation. At the direction of club member and onetime Irish Amateur champion Dr. Billy O'Sullivan and with the support of Bord Fáilte, the old course spawned two "new" courses, now known as Killeen and Mahony's Point. O'Sullivan's energy, imagination, and ambition were the driving forces in developing the Killarney golf environment beyond what anyone else had envisioned.

It was he who made an impassioned plea to create not one new course but two by assigning each course a combination of existing holes and newly constructed ones. Thanks to his foresight, Killarney became the location of two golf courses surrounded by mountains, lakes, and trees, and the results have met with glowing approval since their 1972 completion.

Just two-hours' drive from the anger of cliffs and dunes and winds at Tralee, Waterville, or Ballybunion, the serenity of Killarney might be a welcome tonic for

The devil at #3

Tee marker at Kileen

the Romantic ideal of beauty, writers Sir Walter Scott and William Thackeray were frequent visitors to the area. Today Killarney remains one of the country's top tourist locations.

Atypical of Irish courses, Killeen begins with a high degree of difficulty. Number one is a dogleg infested with water to your right, all the way to the green, and halfway around it. The water continues to play the devil at number three. Be careful. It's not much easier from the regular tees at 170 yards than from the 197-yard tee sitting right out on Lough Leane, one of three contiguous lakes the surrounding mountains sink into.

Number ten might remind you of Pete Dye, though the embankment supports are much smaller than those with which you are familiar if you have played some

the battered player. A land of lush forests, deep-blue lakes, and heather-clad mountains, Killarney has won the hearts of visitors for centuries. For some, it has been a source of inspiration. Believing the region to embody

A panoramic view of the 13th hole, Mahony's Point

A ponderous idea

Pete Dye courses. Number twelve, at 477 yards, plays tougher than many par fives. While reachable in two, its looks can deceive you into thinking you are much farther from the green than you actually are. Listen to your caddie!

Fourteen is one of those rare par fours that from the regular tees can be as demanding as from championship tees, and perhaps more fun. A huge and threatening oak tree juts out from the right rough, insisting that you'd best hit it down the left side, with a fade around the oak if you want a better chance of hitting the green on your next shot: Welcome shot makers.

Eighteen offers its own pleasures. A slight dog leg to the left with a tee shot from a small plateau, it lets you see the entire hole (including the enticing clubhouse, the fifth one they've had) as the backdrop. Depending on how far you hit your drive, you might need a 6 or 7 iron to hit the generously sized green — in easy view of jeering friends in the bar.

Be careful not to let the scenery dull your game. Although undulating hills, flowering shrubs, and sparkling lakes may imply a tamer course than its seaside cousins, Killeen exacts its own price. During the 1991 tournament, several professionals complained that the greens on several holes were unfair. Matters of opinion aside, Killeen holds its own as one of the more beloved courses in Ireland.

The Road from Killarney

To Waterville: The Ring of Kerry

The last time I took this drive was in the early sixties. I was an ambitious advertising executive getting acquainted with my "product": Ireland. Gordon Clark, my opposite number at Bord Fáilte, had decided we should see the Ring of Kerry — that it was among the most appealing, scenic sites in all of Ireland. I'm sure I thought so and said so then, but now, some thirty years later, I realize I was not so awed by that tour as I was by this one.

We left our hotel, the Royal, in the heart of Killarney, bound for Waterville, via the only way you can really get there . . . the Ring. It seemed only moments later that we were in the country amidst shrubs, bushes, trees, and rolling hills. Then we came

A classic home on the road to Waterville

Worship on The Ring

upon something extraordinary: Muckross Abbey, a monastery dating from the nineteenth century. From its lake one can begin to see views of the Shehy and Purple Mountains. Just beyond Muckross, the road stretches out above a portion of the upper Lough Leane set against Macgillycuddy's Reek.

A little farther on and the road begins to wind and climb more. We twisted and turned and suddenly came across an old church at a road junction. It was Sunday and the only parishioners seemed to be a number of

The beautiful sights simply don't stop.

Pastor's gate

marked sheep. With their worship done, they had little to do the rest of the day except dawdle along the road, making sure the drivers stayed within the letter of the speed laws.

We stopped frequently to photograph the ever more exciting views. At one point of interest we came upon a bronze tablet set on a stone, memorializing a road race fatality. The name of the driver has dimmed in my memory, but his courage to race these roads simply astounded me. Once more I was touched by these people who would pay tribute to such spirit.

A sign that points left to Kenmare led us through Molls Gap. It is an imposing array of hills, stone-pocked with no trees to redeem the nearly awesome starkness. There are few homes along the way, and when you do see one, it is usually in the distance and its surroundings

Entering Waterville

are dotted with sheep. As we got closer to Kenmare, however, the homes were nearer the road. Besides being immaculate they are colorful: Some pinks, blues, and even a purple one or two come to mind.

Just short of Kenmare there's another sign that points us north to the Ring and to Blackwater, Sneem, and Waterville.

The first two have population enough to support the occasional bar and pub, some stores, and even a post office. In the center of one town, someone has parked his mule.

Leaving the town, the winding roads start up again as the number of homes diminishes. We enter Parknasilla, pass the entrance to a Great Southern hotel and know our journey to Waterville is more than half over.

Our next town was Castlecove where, as we rounded

yet another sharp bend, we came upon the town church. To the right was a lady with a camera, and directly between her and the church was a rotund young man who had to be the happiest and most quintessentially Irish man I've ever seen. We should have stopped and asked permission to take his picture, but it seemed so obvious and we just didn't have the nerve.

On we drove. We'd barely stopped smiling about our rotund friend when we saw, in the distance, water and a beach and even a billboard advertising Carroll's Cove — all indicators of our proximity to Waterville. No sooner thought than seen, we sidled into the town, which fronts Ballinskelligs Bay with a host of colorful homes and shops. Across the street, as if on a throne, sits the impressive Waterville House, part of the venture that Jack Mulcahy undertook when building the golf course here. It has made many golfers glad they came to this not-easy-to-get-to part of Ireland.

Toward the other end of the town, right at the turn-off to Waterville Club, stands rather proudly the handsome and comfortable Butler Arms. That's kind of your signal to turn left for the "Golf Chumann."

One final thought on our marvelous drive from Killarney to Waterville: Our conversations with more than one person regarding the normal driving time from this place to that. A seemingly sage gentleman told us that however long it takes an Irishman to make whatever journey you're talking about from the Ring, add fifty percent for anyone else. No argument.

ATTITUDE

It has been said that whatever talent one may have, whatever advantage one feels, one must have the right attitude to achieve lofty heights. And perhaps this goes for the young caddie, too, as he aspires to doing an exemplary job and earning a lofty tip.

Take the example of Sean McBride, who as an eleven-year-old was not yet fortunate enough to be considered wise in the ways of the greens at Ballybunion. But he had a good attitude and he tried hard to satisfy his bag that day – an English-born, American-raised, Princeton-educated, golfaholic.

On the rather large fifth green, with the drizzle and temperature falling, and the strident wind letting you know it was there, the golfer and his very ardent caddie studied a putt that must have been sixty feet long. The golfer was in the classic knee-to-the-green posture, and Sean bent at the waist behind him, hands on hips peering studiously over his shoulder down the line of the putt. The golfer turned his head and said, "What do you think, Sean … about eight inches to the left?"

In his Irish brogue, he replied confidently, "Nine, sir."

IRISH FRUGALITY

Although this book focuses on County Kerry, there are many wonderful golfing experiences to be had throughout Ireland. One of my most memorable occurred in the late 1960s at Portmarnock, that gem of the northern coast. To my great delight, I was invited to play with the famous Harry Bradshaw, Portmarnock's professional.

Bradshaw finished second in the 1949 British Open when he was victimized by a freak occurrence and his own misunderstanding of the rules of golf. Dueling the legendary Bobby Locke, Bradshaw hit his drive on the final hole of the tournament into the remains of a broken Coke bottle. He didn't know that the rules allowed him to lift and drop the ball, so he gallantly clubbed the ball from the bottle. He bogeyed the 18th and subsequently lost the championship to Locke. (Locke also won the Open the

Harry Bradshaw and the author, 1967

next year at Troon and in 1952 at Royal Lytham.)

On the morning I arrived at Portmarnock to play with Bradshaw, I was greeted in the pro shop by a short, round man wearing a tweed cap who looked exactly like a caricature of an Irish golfer. He barely nodded and said, "Welcome to Portmarnock." That was Harry Bradshaw.

I immediately followed him and my caddie to the first tee. Bradshaw carried his own bag, which to my astonishment contained only seven clubs! He handed me a scorecard that looked like it had been in his pocket for weeks. When I asked for a pencil, his eyebrows went up and he scurried back to the pro shop to fetch one. It couldn't have been more than two inches long, and the point was no sharper than my thumb.

He asked my handicap. When I replied,

"Three," he said, "You'll get one a side." I was obviously overmatched against one of the greatest Irish golfers of all time.

Through inspiration and luck, I managed to play him even to the 440-yard 17th hole, which was my back-nine shot hole. I hit a career second shot to within eight feet of the pin, while Harry remained short of the green in two. He picked up his ball, skirted the green and said rather stoically, "Let's go to 18."

As I prepared to tee off, he said, "We'll play save-a-stroke."

"What's that?" I asked.

"That's when the pro is one down to the amateur going to the last hole, and the pro gets a shot."

So there I was, a guest playing with a famous pro. Did I dispute his outlandish ploy? Of course not.

I hit a drive down the middle, but Bradshaw pulled his into the deep, left rough. I couldn't help thinking that it served him right. He kept his driver in hand, choked down on the grip, and whacked his second shot toward the green. The ball hit fifty yards short but rolled and rolled and rolled…until it was eight feet from the pin. He lay net one, and I was dead. My shot landed on the green but far from the pin, so, as he had done for me on 17, I graciously conceded his putt.

Save-a-stroke, indeed.

ooooo

We adjourned to the bar where I was introduced to a shantygaff — half beer and half tomato juice. While we waited for a sandwich, I said to Bradshaw, "In America we consider it a privilege to play with the pro, and since we realize we're taking him away from some of his livelihood — like lessons and the shop — we often pay him for his time on the course. Would you mind if I offered you the same?"

He paused for a millisecond before responding with what seemed a very fair price.

After lunch I paid Bradshaw his fee, I paid the bartender and tipped him, and I tipped the waiter, the locker room attendant, and the caddie master. I thanked Harry again and headed for the car.

Before I could leave the parking lot, however, Bradshaw came waddling toward me with an anxious look on his face. Through the open car window he said three never-to-be-forgotten words: "About the pencil…."

Waterville Links Hotel

The Vision That Became Waterville

The story of Waterville Golf Links is probably not as much about a golf course as it is about a man. Born in Dungarvin, Ireland, John A. Mulcahy (Jack, Johnny) immigrated to America, grew up, and made his fortune but never forgot his native land and heritage.

While his early years there in the late sixties and early seventies were spent fishing the waters of the Kenmare and the Atlantic Ocean, where sea trout abounded, he kept an eye on the nine hole links called Waterville, which sat in the shady dunes above Ballinskelligs Bay. At Waterville, he formed his vision of a great golf course.

Mulcahy could afford to bring any designer he wished to Waterville, but instinct bent him to select Eddie Hackett, an Irish designer little known at the time, but who, before his career was over, designed more true links courses than anyone else in history.

Subtle Three

#15, Waterville

The course starts with a hole named Last Easy and progresses to a harder one —number two — and that's the way it goes. The holes begin to toughen up a bit more and gradually the message gets across: You're on one helluva golf course. As you trudge up the ninth, you sense your real test lies just ahead. It comes quickly with a slightly more demanding tee shot than you might have experienced 'til now and a second shot to a slightly concealed green. Then, the eleventh, an exciting par five, has

Resting Place, #17

dunes on both sides of the fairway that seem to tumble most of the way to the green. Hardly visible after your first shot, the green can prove rather severe if your drive does not allow you to approach on your second. (In truth, that's a rare occurrence.) The green bears the name Tranquillity and appropriately so, for it is totally hidden from the rest of the course by majestic but threatening dunes.

The twelfth, a par three of some length from the back tees (200 yards) and modest from the middle (154 yards), is a simple hole, but still demands a good bit of care. A natural chasm between tee and green forms its most outstanding characteristic and secures its place in

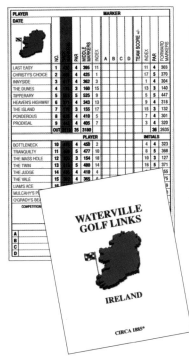

WATERVILLE
GOLF LINKS

IRELAND

CIRCA 1885*

history. When the Irish Catholics' fear of persecution demanded they worship in secret, the chasm served as their place to practice their faith without fear of retribution. Naturally it's called the Mass Hole.

Sixteen, once called "round the bend," is now called Liam's Ace. One of Ireland's longest hitters ever and an extremely fine golfer to boot, Liam Higgins aced this 350-yard hole. He went for the green over a jungle of growth and dunes. As the professional at Waterville, that was not his first try, nor his first time on the green, but his first and the world's last ace at sixteen . . . thus far.

The sheer quality, challenge, and emotion of the seventeenth place it on a par with any other hole in the world. It is nearly 200 yards that can play much longer into a wind and is wild with vegetation that eats errant shots. The green, though appearing rather plain, has a hint of roll, almost imperceptible, that hauntingly speeds up or slows down your putt. Compounding all this is that emotion I spoke of, for here, under the tee box, is where John A. Mulcahy's ashes are interred. It was from this tee, the highest spot in Waterville and on the golf course, that Mulcahy stood with Eddie Hackett and knew he'd make this one of the finest 18-hole

courses made since whoever started golf started golf. This tee is now lovingly known as "Mulcahy's Peak." And the course has been called by *Golf World* "the greatest course built in Great Britain in the last fifty years."

Eighteen will leave you realizing that as a finishing hole it is no slouch. More than one golfer, lengthy off the tee, has played this downhill 582-yarder with three good woods . . . and a wedge. Enough said about that. Having finished the golf course, let's put it in perspective by telling you the course record is 71 since it became eighteen holes in 1972.

What Jack Mulcahy did not know when he committed himself to building the course was that he would bring more to Waterville than a great course. Yes, he brought a lot of people who would help it become famous — golfers like Sam Snead and Ray Floyd and Bob Murphy and celebrities like Tip O'Neil, Telly Savalas, Bob Hope, and Jack Lemmon. But in the end his contribution was far greater: He gave of himself.

On many occasions Jack took youngsters out on the course and helped them with their game. When the number got unmanageable, club professional Liam Higgins jumped in. Such things happened, because Jack set an example. People seemed to want to help as he did. To the kids of the town he was inspirational. Shortly before he died, a group of youngsters he'd treated as family organized a dinner for him and proudly presented Jack a green jacket in gratitude for all that he had taught them. Being the man that he was, he shed a tear at the gesture.

AN AFTERNOON WITH JACK MULCAHY

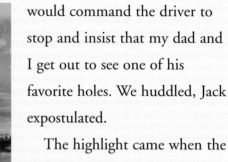

In 1983, I took my dad to Ireland for Father's Day. We drove the length of the Dingle Peninsula to reach Waterville. Jack Mulcahy, the larger-than-life Irish-American who built the place, was there to greet us.

Because of the foul weather — it was blowing fifty miles per hour and raining sideways — Jack welcomed us into the Waterville House, where a peat fire burned in the drawing room and where we sipped whiskey to warm ourselves.

Jack insisted that we see the links, his pride and joy, even if we couldn't play it. The three of us jumped into the back seat of his spacious black Daimler, and Jack instructed the driver to head for the first tee.

Incredibly, the car did not sink into the grass. It glided along the fairways without leaving a mark, this despite the torrential rain. Every so often Jack would command the driver to stop and insist that my dad and I get out to see one of his favorite holes. We huddled, Jack expostulated.

The highlight came when the car lurched to a stop below a flattened dune called Mulcahy's Peak, the highest point on the course. I followed Jack on hands and knees to the pinnacle, where the great man looked likes Moses calling for the tablet as he waved his arms around in the howling wind, his thin, white windbreaker snapping about his ample girth.

My dad and I were very, very happy to return to the comforts of Waterville House, though the chauffeur-driven tour of one of Ireland's greatest links (with its patriarch as our guide) is one we'll never forget!

— BRIAN MCCALLEN,
Senior Editor, Golf Magazine, *September 1996*

THE HEARTBEAT OF WATERVILLE

Noel Cronin was an automobile driver in the small town of Waterville, County Kerry, Ireland, population five hundred. Whenever "Johnny" Jack Mulcahy came to town to visit his golf course, Noel was his driver. And likewise, he was the exclusive driver for golf course designer Eddie Hackett when he was in Waterville.

When a group of Irish-Americans bought the Waterville properties from Mulcahy, they approached Cronin to manage the golf course. Noel knew about greens and fairways and grass, and he knew plenty about golf (he has a single digit handicap), but he had never managed anything other than himself . . . and that none too well, to hear him tell it.

But nine years later, he is still secretary/manager of the Waterville course, and in 1996 he was named Secretary/Manager of the Year for all of Ireland by the Irish Golf Links Tour Operators Association.

This unassuming, typically-Irish looking gentleman (short, stout, weathered face) is the per-sonification of manners, humility, pride, and enthusiasm. When he speaks from behind the cluttered desk in his office, it's as clear and artful as if he had prepared his comments for delivery from a podium.

"Kids shouldn't play only golf," he philosophizes, "no matter how strong their desire. Learning to win and lose on a team prepares them better to win and lose as individuals on the golf course."

Another gem from Noel Cronin reinforced our notion that the Irish play golf to enjoy it as much as to master it: "We Irish quite often get as much pleasure from missing a putt as we do

from making one." And then a smile crinkled across his face, and you knew that somewhere Johnny Mulcahy was pleased.

Ceann Sibéal

When we organized this trip to Ireland, we didn't plan on playing "Dingle," the common name for Ceann Sibéal (the Gaelic for "Sybil's Head"). But in talking with caddies, golfers, and even club managers, we were pointed in the direction of Dingle with more than one "You ought to try it."

Getting there was part of the fun. "Take this road and that one . . . go through Dingle . . . just a bit farther, a few miles (turned out to be an Irish few; it was actually 10 miles), take a right turn at the second road through Ballyferriter and then go over the bridge . . . you'll see plenty of signs."

Gridlock. *The road to Ballybunion might include the surprise of a delay for cows going from field to feeding. But you won't mind it a bit; it's brief and the manner of their herder is inevitably concerned and charming.*

TOYOTA
Ifreann
Poll 9
Pár 4 Méadar 390
Treoir 1

Those were the directions. Following them wasn't all that easy. As expected on Irish roads, we paused once for a herd of cows and their gracious herders. On we traveled through the immaculate towns of Ballheige and Camp and then through Dingle (a town with 1,500 people and 50 bars!) as we sought signs to take us to the golf course.

Once past the town, we completely lost sight of anything resembling a directional sign to the course. Then suddenly, we were in Ballyferriter where we reluctantly (men are that way about asking directions) asked and were told "straight up the road, second right, over the bridge (what a bridge!), and you'll see it." And we did. We wondered what leprechaunish imagination conjured up the signs we'd been told to look for. If they are there, they are rather cunningly concealed.

On first look the golf course appeared to be an understated resort, comprised of smallish houses, cottage-size, where people could come to rest after a day of golf and sightseeing. We noticed right away that the language of the club is Irish (Gaelic). Dingle is "Gaeltacht," one of the rapidly diminishing areas in Ireland where Irish is spoken by significant numbers. Everyone at the club speaks Irish and all signage is in the native tongue — even the scorecard. (Of course, they speak English, too.)

We also noticed the tremendous hospitality of the place. At the pro shop we took a couple of Kit Kat bars for the course. When we asked the price, they insisted we were their guests. Talk about a warm welcome!

We soon headed for the first tee with our caddies, Michael and Cormack. It took only moments for us to observe that one was the outgoing type and the other a bit reserved, but both made us feel they were glad we'd come to their course. They turned out to be an important part of the enjoyment and told us what we needed to

Approaching the Three Sisters

know and much of interest about the area.

One particularly amusing incident involved Michael berating Cormack for what he felt was a bit of bad advice. It happened at the thirteenth hole when our "big hitter" (and the highest handicapped of our threesome) wanted to cut the corner of the dog leg by flying the ball over a rather formidable fence. "You can make it," said Cormack. With barely more than a stage whisper, Michael uttered, "No way." Challenged by the quiet comment, our big hitter tried. And tried again. As we headed down the fairway (he'd hit a sen-

sible fifth stroke down the middle), we could hear Michael rubbing it in to Cormack with great relish.

The course may not be a Ballybunion or Waterville or Tralee, but it is, according to some, "mesmerizing." Pushed against the sea, it is the westernmost course in Europe. With waves crashing against the cliffs below, swales and hollows complicating every shot, the Three Sisters looming in the distance, and wind wreaking havoc, the course can defy its docile appearance. The designers, Eddie Hackett and Christy O'Connor, Jr., made smart use of the land that slopes down to the sea by creating an exciting mixture of uphill and downhill holes. As you move over this course, you will shake your head in wonder at the raw beauty of the landscape, so different from other places in Ireland.

The first hole, a nice start, is a slightly downhill par four on which a brook comes into play on your approach shot. The second, an excellent par three of 200 yards, has well-placed bunkers and undulation that demands you take a good look. The holes that follow range from good to fair, but never mind. When you get to number nine you have a beauty: 427 yards up a fairly serious grade to another well-bunkered green. Don't plan on reaching it unless you're long; do plan on one putt if you want a par.

The second nine commences with the westernmost hole in all of Ireland — a real toughie. It, like the second, is right at two hundred yards with an extremely wide but shallow and raised green that is difficult to see, except for the right front corner which features a bunker and bailout area. The green sits slightly higher than the tee and the flag this day proved the grounds superintendent is evil, for it appeared to be almost as far west as New York. It's an intimidating shot, yet "big hitter" got it on to ten feet.

Number ten indicates what is to come. There isn't a hole on the back nine that could be called dull. You'll particularly enjoy eighteen, a 500-yarder, beautifully bunkered on both sides of the fairway and complemented with a green that any designer would be proud to have sculpted.

Dingle is indeed a breathtaking sight and what better way to illustrate this than to quote the authors of *Links of Heaven*:

It is all cliffs and surf and haunting desolation. On a stormy day you feel like you are at the end of the earth.

Of course this was the end of the earth for many centuries, at least as far as Europeans were concerned. The remains of ring forts of Irish kings dot the surrounding landscape. There are also several impressive Christian ruins dating back a millennium or so, a reminder that Irish monasteries were the last refuge of Christian learning during Europe's Dark Ages. Just off the shore are the Blasket Islands. Though unpopulated today, these islands once produced some of the best writers of Gaelic literature.

We were gratified we'd played the course and mused that it really fit two scenarios: (1) as a course for people who want golf in Ireland but don't want to be as seriously challenged as at Ballybunion and (2) as a course for the people who come to Ireland to play the deservedly famous Ballybunion, Waterville, and Tralee but might enjoy a lighter fare as a "break" on their golf tour. It has been said that visitors often think of Ceann Sibéal as a kind of refuge — how nice these days when escape is so fleeting!

A WORD ABOUT EDDIE HACKETT

Eddie Hackett was a warm, talented, humble, respected, loved, and venerable Irish gentleperson, who designed more links courses than any other man, anyplace in the world . . . and he did it in one country. But he did so much more. He is almost the patron saint of Irish golf, having nurtured the inclination of, some say, half of Ireland's golf population to take up the game.

He was always a one-man band; no partners, no employees, yet he kept moving, regardless of his age, doing one great course after the other.

He was never the kind of golf course architect-designer who was interested in observing and absorbing the topography and strategies and intricacies of other courses, but rather, in his own words, his genius and success lay with the philosophy that he worked to "dress up whatever the Good Lord provides."

Between the Hills, Dooks, #14

Dooks is a golf course that's really quite special. Little known because it has not been documented as have the likes of Waterville and Ballybunion, it nevertheless cuts its own outstanding swath as a site which offers perhaps the most beautiful surroundings of any golf course in the west of Ireland. Dooks is laid out on one of three stretches of sand dunes at the head of Dingle Bay. And to the uninformed it comes of more than passing interest that the Killarney, Dingle and Slieve Mish Mountains are all easily visible, and oh yes, the mighty MacGillycuddy Reeks too!

Dooks

Per ardua ad astra 18 89

We arrived at Dooks without having called ahead and wondered what to expect. We knew the manager's name, Michael Shanahan, and asked after him. (There is no pro.) In a few moments he appeared and ushered us into the dining room. It was pleasantly aged with a proper bar at one end and equipped with an equally proper staff who allowed us a moment to sit before taking our drink orders and inquiring whether we would be staying to eat. That done, Mr. Shanahan joined us and spent over an hour giving us a colorful narrative of the history of the club.

Dooks was the first golf club in all of Kerry. It was named for the dunes, for "Dooks" is Gaelic for "sandbank" which is exactly what it is built on, at the head of Dingle Bay. Like Lahinch, it attributes its early development to the military officers who decided "to use the beautiful dunes for better purposes than firing guns." They encouraged the local gentry to become involved and showed them the finer points of the game over the then-impromptu course. That was in 1889.

In the years that followed, the Great Southern Railway Hotel at Caragh Lake promoted the course as a local attraction. According to the Dooks book, the club became "a reflection of the lifestyle of British ascendancy: both men and women enjoyed the course and came to Dooks from the lake, and Tralee and Killarney by train

and 'pony trap' for weekends of fun and golf competition. They competed for prizes of cash and silver, or both. And in the style they were accustomed to, members enjoyed the afternoon teas and social amenities that were so much a part of the era."

As time passed the golf became more competitive; trophies representing specific, and later to become traditional, events were established. The members likewise became more serious and began to embrace the club with loyalty and something near affection.

Member Nora Kelliher contributed these warm remembrances of the course to its centennial book:

Left: *Lady Gordon, the Captain*
Below: *A view over #2*

Take the break, right. *Irish caddies seem to have earned the implicit respect that encourages visitors to seek and heed their advice and wisdom. Depending on your manner and mode of play, that advice may be gentle or tart…but it's almost always right. Almost.*

"In the mid-thirties when I first went there, Dooks was a short nine-hole links. Most of the holes had lovely turf, but a few were boggy and gorse abounded. In early summer the greens were good, surrounded by wire to keep out the sheep, which helped keep the fairways in trim. I remember well the short fourth hole — now I believe the thirteenth — with the basin-shaped green, where an ace was very possible and anything from a birdie to a horrible double bogey fairly common."

In 1970, the members decided to expand the original nine-hole layout to eighteen. It could have been a monumental mess. Because the club had only a small cash reserve, the nine-person committee appointed to oversee construction decided to do the work themselves, assigning each member of the committee a hole to design. (This might well mean that a club of rather small membership

may have had the largest design staff in the history of the game!) The members did all the work — from finding materials to using those materials for the bunkers they dug and the greens they shaped and the fairways they contoured. They managed the entire renovation for less than $4,000, and what's more, they created an excellent course in the process.

The history of Dooks, like the course, has been shaped by its unusual and thoughtful membership. Two episodes illustrate this point. In 1921, the club appointed Lady Edith Gordon as captain. At the time, granting such an important position to a woman was a revolutionary action for an Irish club. Then some sixty years later, the club again showed its mettle by deftly handling a public relations crisis. Accused by a local environmentalist group of threatening the breeding grounds of the Natterjack toad, the club changed its plans. "There'll be none of that," said the members, and then, showing their verve, they built new breeding grounds and adopted the toad as its logo. When the members of Dooks encounter an obstacle, they always find a creative way around it. Their motto, *Per ardua as astra* (Through hard work to the stars), seems both to define and to inspire them.

Dooks starts out with a trying hole. Not only is the tee shot demanding and blind, but the green is tightly guarded. Number two, which is not much more than a wedge shot, uphill with a trap in exactly the wrong place, is no cinch either. The next few holes are fairly straightforward, except for number six which is both beautiful to play (you kind of bank your shot off the right side of the fairway) and to view, as you look to the north over the bay. And seven is called "Dr. Bill's," in honor of its designer Dr. William O'Sullivan of Killarney fame. It's short in length but not in style. Nine is a deceivingly good par three.

The back nine continues in the style of the front, working its way through the dunes. Miss Kelliher has already told you about number thirteen. Fourteen and sixteen present gorse-enhanced challenges. Number eighteen will find you, if your first two shots are satisfying, with an approach to "knowhere," as it's been described. When you've finished and are enjoying a "jar" in the bar, we're sure this hole may well be the main subject of your discussions about the course. However, more of your discussions and reflections on Dooks will focus on the tranquillity of the place and the magnificent

views, and perhaps, more than anything else, the sheer hospitality that blankets Ireland and seems even more poignant here.

Can you imagine . . . Mr. Shanahan even bought our lunch!

Stoic

*The impassive cliffs protruding into the Shannon Estuary, and viewed here from
Ballybunion Castle, form a natural shelter for Ballybunion Bay with its marvelous
beach and surfing area, in this quiet though buoyant seaside resort.*

Ballybunion

The town of Ballybunion seems to gently grab you by the lapels with its amalgam of delights: main street and its plethora of pubs and bars and restaurants and shops. And whatever the place of business, when you enter, you become part of the owner's universe. Notable locations for sightseeing include the Heritage Museum, the Sisters of Mercy Convent School, Knockanore Hill, and the Marconi wireless station (site of the first east-west wireless transmission). For the visitor not so interested in biking or walking tours, the beach, the Shannon River Estuary, and Ballybunion Castle are quiet retreats.

LANGUAGE BARRIER

An American golfer was wandering through the pro shop at Ballybunion when he noticed a Footjoy display that was grandiosely verbal about some new kind of socks. When the alert young assistant in the pro shop asked if he could be of help, the American posed a couple of questions about this apparent new wonder sock. Satisfied with the young man's explanation, he said, "Okay, I'll try a pair."

The still alert young man responded briskly, "Oh, sir, customers are only permitted to buy them … not try them."

Rainbow Row

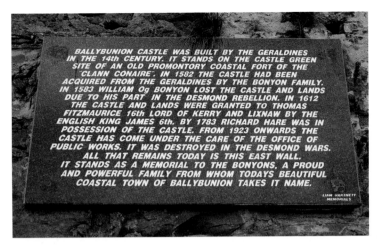

BALLYBUNION CASTLE WAS BUILT BY THE GERALDINES
IN THE 14th CENTURY. IT STANDS ON THE CASTLE GREEN
SITE OF AN OLD PROMONTORY COASTAL FORT OF THE
'CLANN CONAIRE'. IN 1582 THE CASTLE HAD BEEN
ACQUIRED FROM THE GERALDINES BY THE BONYON FAMILY.
IN 1583 WILLIAM Og BONYON LOST THE CASTLE AND LANDS
DUE TO HIS PART IN THE DESMOND REBELLION. IN 1612
THE CASTLE AND LANDS WERE GRANTED TO THOMAS
FITZMAURICE 16th LORD OF KERRY AND LIXNAW BY THE
ENGLISH KING JAMES 6th. BY 1783 RICHARD HARE WAS IN
POSSESSION OF THE CASTLE. FROM 1923 ONWARDS THE
CASTLE HAS COME UNDER THE CARE OF THE OFFICE OF
PUBLIC WORKS. IT WAS DESTROYED IN THE DESMOND WARS.
ALL THAT REMAINS TODAY IS THIS EAST WALL.
IT STANDS AS A MEMORIAL TO THE BONYONS, A PROUD
AND POWERFUL FAMILY FROM WHOM TODAYS BEAUTIFUL
COASTAL TOWN OF BALLYBUNION TAKES IT NAME.

LIAM HARTNETT
MEMORIALS

Ballybunion Castle is almost a monument to itself.

Promontory

The anticipation begins long before you arrive. It is impossible not to be captivated by the idea of playing what many consider the world's greatest golf course.

Although the history of the club is a bit sketchy, some facts are known. An article published August 19, 1893, in the *Limerick Chronicle* announced the formation of the Ballybunion Club. Noted in the text are specifics such as officers and a description of the twelve-hole course "which may be increased should the members so wish." The identity of the original designer is not listed, however, and to this day remains a mystery.

The course entered the modern era and received its present form in 1937, when architect Tom Simpson and his assistant Molly Gourlay polished the facets of this shining jewel. A word first about this man, so unlike his peers. He was flamboyant, affluent, and, though a lawyer by degree, obsessed with the desire to design golf courses. His eccentricities seemed to carry over into his selection of a female assistant — Molly Gourlay. But

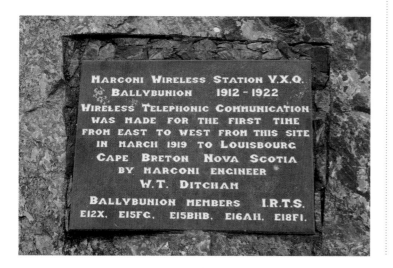

The bar in the Marine Links Hotel in Ballybunion is called the "Hook and Socket." All golfers know what a hook is, but we questioned the meaning of socket. "In Ireland," we were told, "it's not polite to say it aloud." (It's a shank.)

she should have been no surprise. A respected Curtis Cup player and an English ladies champion, she certainly had the proper credentials for the job.

Their philosophies blended beautifully. Their common understanding had three tenets: (1) The absence of artificiality is the most important feature of a course, (2) Each green must be unique, and (3) A course must be a true test for the fine player and at the same time enjoyable for the player with average skills. As at Muirfield, Cruden Bay, Chantilly (France), and Royal Antwerp (Belgium), these ideas shaped all of Simpson's courses.

For all its grandeur, Ballybunion persisted as a virtual unknown until 1971, when renowned golf writer Herbert Warren Wind gushed "Ballybunion revealed itself to be nothing less than the finest seaside course I have ever seen" in the pages of the *New Yorker*. To be certain, Wind's endorsement put Ballybunion, which he

SMALL WORLD, TOUGH COURSE

And there was the night our group went to a pub in Ballybunion. Upon being seated, one of our recalcitrants spotted a table of eight middle-aged, presumably Irish ladies, also presumably out on the town for the evening. He suggested we send over a bottle of wine.

Done.

Ten minutes later, one of the ladies approached and asked, "Whom do we thank for the wine?"

I immediately responded, "Nobody 'til you tell us where you got that American accent." To which she responded that she had come from San Francisco twenty-six years earlier when she had married the course superintendent at Cashen (the "new" course at Ballybunion).

Instantly, one of our group said to her, "Tell him to lighten up!"

The agony of one club short

JUST AN ARRANGEMENT

In Ireland there is a financial assistance system for those unfortunates who can't find work. It's called "dole assistance" and is similar to our welfare program.

A somewhat mischievous caddie at Ballybunion got himself "living on the dole," despite the rules that if you're on the system you can't be earning money elsewhere, which of course he did by caddying.

The authorities caught on to his little miscarriage of justice and, being aware of his low regard for the rules and the truth, decided the best way to confront him was with photographs of him "at work."

Hiding among the dunes of the course, they got their picture and on the next appointed day for him to pick up his "dole," they challenged him with the evidence — the picture of him actually caddying.

"Oh, that," he said. "That's me, all right, caddying for my friend from America. You see, we have an arrangement: Any time he comes here, I caddie for him, and whenever I go there, he caddies for me."

Soliloquy

had discovered by accident, quite literally on the golfing map. Ten years later, Tom Watson would pick up the torch and seal the fate of the course. With statements from Watson, such as, "After playing Ballybunion for the first time, a man would think the game originated here," the course instantly became *the* golfing destination in Ireland.

So what is it about Ballybunion that makes it so remarkable? I think most enthusiasts would attribute its greatness to how it follows the natural flow of the land. The experience of Ballybunion is something that will not leave you. It is so memorable, so distinct. It's the kind of golf course you must never play just once — you must play it twice, at the least. As Herbert Warren Wind wrote: "A tourist driving through Switzerland is staggered by its prodigal beauty; around the bend from the most

Ballybunion sanctuary, overlooking the estuary

Coming to Town

The subtle colors, the usually uncrowded streets still speak of the years gone by,

and the quiet pulse of today, in Ballybunion.

TWO OF THE BEST
ABOUT ONE OF THE BEST

⌇⌇

Herbert Warren Wind has made himself known and appreciated throughout the world with words. Tom Watson has done the same thing with golf clubs.

Both have deified Ballybunion.

Herb Wind recently had a book dedicated to him as "the Bob Jones of Golf Writers." That says it all, as do his writings . . . and no place better than in a 1971 article he wrote about Ballybunion. His words then, describing the course, stand up as well today as when penned:

ABOUT LINKSLAND COURSES: "It is only when the golfer gets out onto a linksland course that he discovers, to his amazement, that it is filled with great holes, all the more appealing since the strategic features were molded by nature instead of a bulldozer."

ABOUT WHAT IS *NOW* THE SIXTH HOLE BUT WAS THE FIRST WHEN THIS WAS WRITTEN: "From the tee the hole appears to be a rather banal par four, but when upon reaching that point in the fairway where an adequate drive would finish, you study the long narrow green, a medium iron away, and the convolutions of the land in the green area, your assessment changes radically. It is then you perceive a formidable arresting hole."

WHERE HE SPEAKS OF THE SECOND (NOW SEVENTH) AND SIXTH (NOW ELEVENTH) HOLES: "From the tee the entire hole is visible and, as if this were not an exhilarating enough prospect, farther in the distance, at the end of a tight valley, between two rows of sand hills, the eye takes in the minute green of another dazzling cliff-side hole, the sixth. I breathed it all in slowly, wondering first to myself and then aloud who the architect was who had the genius to use the duneland in such a thrilling way."

The more I read Herb Wind, the more I believe he also should have been a painter.

Now, Tom Watson's golf world is, of course, quite different from Herb Wind's. He has gone far beyond being merely an almost unparalleled success as a touring golf professional. He has been an exemplary citizen, recognizing the need for community involvement, and just as important, backing up that recognition with matching time, mind, and money to help the young people in his community through golf.

But back to his thoughts about Ballybunion, in which two of his statements are so simple, and given thought, so obvious, but so profound:

"After playing Ballybunion for the first time, a man would think the game originated here."

And, "Ballybunion is a course which many golf architects should live and play before they build golf courses."

Northern Gold

Renaissance

If you think the 7th hole is a great one now, you should have seen it before the sea got

to it. No dog leg…just a straight-away par 4, a bit shorter than its replacement,

but with a near terrifying shot into a green that peers not too cautiously over

the precipice. Pity the sea won out; however, the stalwarts of the original,

determined to see it righted, are doing that now!

Above: *#8, one of the best* Below: *Ballybunion's new world clubhouse*

wondrous view he has ever beheld he comes upon a view that surpasses it and so on and on, endlessly. Ballybunion is something like that. I do not mean to suggest there are vistas that put the one from the second tee to shame — there aren't — but there is a correspondence in the way one stirring hole is followed by another and another."

In the many years and hundreds of courses I've played, I cannot recall one that has as many terrifying tee shots as Ballybunion. The intimidation begins at number one. As

No Relief, *#7 green from 9th tee*

You may still be perplexed as you look back at the 7th green from the 9th tee. It's not an easy tee shot hole, and the second shot is even tougher. Then, once on the green you could be at the mercy of the green's keeper, for there are some scary putts . . . and some scarier ones: Hopefully his mood was good when making pin placements.

How many courses start at a graveyard?

you look down a pleasant fairway (pleasant if you don't mind the cemetery at the right), you see only the pair of bunkers Tom Simpson positioned to eat up errant shots. (By the way, the bunkers, immediately after installment, were aptly named Mrs. Simpson.)

Number eight is a hole rarely lauded but which I consider one of the best. It is listed at 137 yards and calls for an eight or nine iron or sometimes even a wedge because it's below you a bit. But then, of course, the pin position impacts your choice, too. It may be easier into the wind than with it. The right rear part of the green falls sharply into the rough. The front right is guarded by a small bunker, and on the left, almost center, part of the green is a mound that tongues its

WHAT CAN MASSAGE PARLORS AND GOLFERS HAVE TO DO WITH EACH OTHER?

You've probably heard a lot of stories during your life about massage parlors, but chances are you've never heard one quite like this. A local man in Ballybunion, an excellent golfer, had never won two particular events at his club. He had come oh-so-close, but something always seemed to happen to prevent him from winning. Finally, he went to a "massage parlor" in the Golf Hotel, and he won event No. 1. He went again and won event No. 2!

A massage parlor? Actually it's a golf clinic, but at first glance the advertising leads you to the impression that it's really a massage parlor. The leaflet I picked up for the O'Conlon Golf Clinic offered:

MASSAGE (SPORTS)

Back and shoulders	*10 pounds*
Full body	*20 pounds*
Legs and thighs	*10 pounds*
Golf psychology	*20 pounds*
Sauna	*4 pounds*
Golfer's special:	*23 pounds*

This really sounded strange. Was it a ruse? Could it be worth a laugh or two? No way. Veronica O'Conlon is one serious, professional lady. She's also quite charming.

Several years ago, Ms. O'Conlon, the licensed proprietor, resided in Britain where she was in "care" work — helping people who needed counseling. One day a friend invited her to lunch at her golf club. Veronica didn't play golf but she reasoned she wasn't going for golf, she was going for lunch. She came away from a long lunch with an awareness of golfers she'd never had before; they seemed to have larger-than-life egos and an arrogance she simply didn't understand. She wondered why.

Being both a studious and ambitious person, Veronica delved into a study of golf psychology

and learned how much of a mind game golf can be. She studied the game further and discovered that while the mechanics are not all that difficult to absorb and implement, that "implementation" becomes a lot more difficult under pressure.

She realized, of course, that the mind must be free to work on the mechanics, and since the muscles are what make the mechanics work, they too must be properly conditioned. So, it stands to reason that you condition the mind through "message" and the muscles through "massage." Thus began an unusual and successful business.

When asked if she is a golfer, she says she only recently started playing, but not because of her business. "After all," she reasoned, "a male gynecologist can treat women without having had a baby."

The Shrine. *If you put all your golf course fantasies into one, if you believe in the ultimate for scenery, sense and challenge, then standing here, and looking there . . . over the green, down the fairway, across to the sea, you'll know Balllybunion has it all.*

way onto the green, causing you a moment of thought if your tee shot is on the short side of the mound and the pin on the long side. If the pin is center or back-right and your ball has found the front bunker by chance, don't aim for the pin. Aim for the tongue and let the ball climb it, and once over its crest, the ball will sneak its way toward the hole. However, if your tee shot is a bit over the right side of the green, no matter where the pin is, play your pitch past the pin and let the left shoulder of the green act as a backboard. It sounds totally unfair,

but isn't. It just requires some thinking, which all of us can do more of on any golf course.

The ninth hole is a bit of a dog. No, it's a son of a bitch! You need position and length from your drive, and those are not easily achieved. You also inevitably need a pretty lengthy second shot that has to get past the front third of the green or else the steepness of that green could cause your ball to roll back as many as thirty feet from the green, leaving you sixty feet short of the pin. It doesn't seem fair. But then, whoever said golf was fair!

Down the Chute, *#11*

A good look at Cashen

Let it suffice to say that Tom Watson calls number eleven the greatest. (In difficulty it compares with number seventeen at St. Andrews.) Despite being a single-digit player most of my life, I haven't parred that one in more than a dozen tries. Once when I was on a golfing tour with fifteen friends, one member of the group suggested everyone put a punt (a pound) into a pool for the next day's round with the understanding that whoever parred eleven would win. No one parred. Enough said.

Finally, eighteen. It's too bad that it comes at the end of the round (it used to be number thirteen and you could forget it by the time you got to eighteen). Your drive is toward an enormous cross bunker, which is in fact a 1,000-year-old midden, which the dictionary defines as a trash heap. This one has stones and bones and shells dating from the fifth century in it. Regardless of whether you're right, left, or short of it, you're left with a blind shot to a green that is especially memorable: shoulders and deep grass on three sides and a pin that doesn't become visible until you're quite near it.

Let's deal with Cashen, the second and new course at Ballybunion, for a moment, for it is a course worthy of some comment, i.e. it's better than its reputation. That reputation may have been built out of the course's original presentation which some players thought was gimmicky; "Mickey Mouse" others would say. But since then much work has been done to take advantage of its topography, rather than use that topography to trick it up. Still further, Cashen may well have suffered by being constantly compared with the "Old," or because pundits like Peter Doberreiner and the builder Robert Trent Jones both said about it that it was built on the most beautiful linksland site ever. The expectations were just too great, and the course being so new, it couldn't keep up with the "Old," not yet anyway. Many courses of great character like the Old Course can be played once and most of the holes long remembered. But to play it once would be a pity: Tell friends who are headed for Ballybunion to play it no less than twice. You'll better remember all the holes and the special gifts of nature that make it so great.

ANOTHER PERSPECTIVE

Some friends announced they were going to Ireland for a golf vacation. Being the fanatic that I am, I immediately planned much of their trip and told them exactly where to play. I sent them to dream courses like Portmarnock, Waterville, Tralee, and Ballybunion.

Three weeks later I saw them again and asked about the trip. They told me they'd had a wonderful time — the sights, the shops, and the golf courses.

"And what about Ballybunion?" I said. "Wasn't it every bit as wonderful as I told you?"

The woman answered, "I hated it. No trees."

Long Walk. *Only in Ireland might you find three par 3s in a stretch of four holes. But it would be tough to find one better than #15 at about two hundred yards. With its two levels and the contouring of the green and its immediate surroundings, your walk toward it can be a worrisome one, for even a well-struck shot cannot always be seen 'til you pass that last large dune on the left.*

MODESTY BECOMES

One afternoon in Ballybunion we strolled the town and ambled our way slightly off the main drag. We came to Church Road, and while it's residential, a sign at the intersection promised us a "shopping opportunity" — a delightful shop that displayed a myriad of items indigenous, of course, to the country.

The proprietress left us alone but was easily within earshot for any questions. Mine was about a cloche-type hat (for Miss Murphy, of course). I asked that fairly typical and not too intelligent question, "What is it?" knowing perfectly well what it was but wanting to get a handle on the price. She took one from my hands, put it on to demonstrate that it was a hat, and smiled pertly.

It looked nice, and so, given to impulse, I commented, "That looks nice on you."

Her response: "Of course it does. Why else would I put it on!"

Ireland seems to have more different looking windows than anywhere in the world. Perhaps that's because of the legend that every one of them has its own "signature" lace curtains.

The Fourth Estate Commentary

I asked some friends in the fourth estate to give me their personal thoughts about Ballybunion. Here they are:

FROM JERRY TARDE, EDITOR, *GOLF DIGEST:*

Many of us operate under the mistaken belief that the best golf in the world is in Scotland, when, of course, it's been in Ireland all the time. The dunes are steeper, the wind is stiffer, the grass is greener — and the people are just plain nicer than anywhere else you've been.

And the best of the lot is Ballybunion. Where else can you play blind shots walking through a cemetery with a green-haired caddie in the teeming rain, and enjoy yourself so much?

FROM GEORGE PEPER, EDITOR IN CHIEF, *GOLF MAGAZINE:*

Ballybunion — the very word sends chills up the spine. It sounds like the site of a Napoleonic battle. Indeed, this wild and magnificent stretch of Irish coastline would be an ideal place to fend off any army of invaders. But it's an even better place to play golf.

FROM AL BARKOW, NOTED GOLF JOURNALIST:

You want to know what the luck o' the Irish really is? Not only that they have Ballybunion, but that it's at their doorstep. Then again, having to travel a great distance to get there makes for a grand Rite of Passage. Or Passage Rite. Anyway, it is the quintessential expression of golf's most universal charm — its geography. All talk of a magnificent, fortuitous conjunction of land and sea begins with Ballybunion. That it's also near the headwater of the Guinness River is not such a bad thing, either.

FROM ROBIN MCMILLAN, EDITOR, *MET GOLFER MAGAZINE:*

Being Scottish, I don't particularly enjoy playing golf in hot summer weather, but I don't remember playing in worse weather than at Ballybunion. The wind was howling so badly out to sea — the opposite of the prevailing direction — that the clouds seemed to be traveling faster than our golf balls. The rain was so heavy that it rendered our rain suits feckless and made gripping a golf club as easy as gripping water — which is sort of what we were doing.

But we soldiered on, chasing our golf balls along between the dunes, and sometimes up and over them. I don't think I recorded a single par — and not that many bogeys, either — after a sandy on the first hole, until we reached the eighteenth. There, after a perfectly struck 6-iron approach (blind, of course), I stood over a ten-foot putt for birdie — at last! — with water cascading from the tip of my nose onto the top of my ball. And all I could think was, "Well, I guess my head's in the right position." Then I left it short.

What D'ya Think?

"Go ahead sucker . . . go for it!" What Tom Watson calls one of the toughest holes
in the world might call for a lay up or two, depending on how well you hit the
drive, and second . . . and the wind and your caddie; #11 . . . wow!

FROM MARK BROWN, GOLF JOURNALIST

The venerable old course at Ballybunion can be described as nothing less than spectacular. Without question, it is the most exhilarating venue of golf in the British Isles. With its massive sand dunes tossing and turning with reckless abandon — and plunging well over one hundred feet to the waters of the Shannon Estuary — Bally-bunion offers the golfer some of the most magnificent golf and vistas in the world. The brilliant routing of the holes through the valleys between the splendid dunes and out to the sea provides one of the most awe-inspiring tests of shot-making skill in the kingdom of golf.

FROM MATT SULLIVAN, EDITOR, *LINKS MAGAZINE:*

The anticipation begins to mount the night before. You're going to where all golfers dream of playing, a place you know will become one of the most special on earth to you. The wild and primitive dunescape, the massive dunes and panoramic views — the kind of terrain the game was invented to be played on.

Exhilarating yet formidable. Majestic yet ferocious. I can still see it vividly.

FROM CHRISTY O'CONNOR, SR.:

Anyone who breaks par here is playing better than he is able.

OBVIOUS!

〜

The tee shot at No. 16 at Ballybunion is aimed at a fairway that's almost at right angles to the tee. If you hit a good one, you then have your back to the sea as you face the green and a chance to go for it ... even though it's a par five. A rather proud and somewhat vain man who'd been trying to prove his prowess all day had hit a prodigious tee shot which left him maybe 220 yards from the green. He stood over the ball, back to the sea, hands on hips, peering towards the green, and asked his caddie one ponderous question after the other: "What's to the left?" "What's to the right?" And finally, when he asked, "What's behind?" the caddie said, "The sea, sir."

IRELAND'S LOVELY LINKS

It was on the eighteenth tee at Ballybunion, high on a windy cliff overlooking the Shannon Estuary, that I experienced my most terrifying moment in golf.

Actually, "terrifying" may be a bit strong. "Blockheaded" is closer. Indeed, in the last year or so I've pulled some stupendously stupid stunts on the golf course: I played my opponent's ball in a sudden-death playoff; I missed a ten-foot birdie putt while playing with Nancy Lopez in front of a thousand people (I left it short); and I staged a show at the seventeenth tee of the new Tournament Players Club that was so mortifying I can't bear to recount it. But none of those exploits caused me the embarrassment I felt at Ballybunion.

My plight was simple: I was out of golf balls. Out of golf balls for the first time in my life. Out of golf balls with one hole to go on one of the finest courses in Creation. Out of golf balls, with the club secretary, the club pro, and the club captain peering at me inquisitively from a window in the distant clubhouse.

I was not playing alone. My good wife, Libby, was with me — and she had run out of balls two holes earlier. We had begun the day with a seemingly safe supply of a dozen, but the high winds and daunting design of Ballybunion had reduced us to one apiece by the turn. Playing carefully, I had survived through the first half of the seventeenth, where a good drive left me an approach with a 9 iron — a 9 iron that, I shortly discovered, should have been a half wedge.

We searched the brush in back of the green for nearly a quarter hour before I said, "Let's go in. I'll fake a limp and tell the boys I fell into one of their pot bunkers."

Then I got a break. After walking roughly fifty yards up the fairway I glimpsed a speck of white eight feet up the sand hill that looms along the right side of the hole. Fifteen seconds later I clutched a battered, smiling Dunlop 65. Fifte minutes later I sank a thirty-foot putt on the home hole, to save par, and face.

The experience, though briefly harrowing, was somehow typical of Ireland, where magnificent scenery and rugged courses blend with blessed Irish Luck to provide some of the most enjoyable golf in the world.

— *George Peper, Editor in Chief,* GOLF Magazine

Temptress. *#10 at Ballybunion is a tease. It takes a well sculpted tee shot (use a driver and you could repent). Whatever you use, your second shot, assuming your first is ok, demands a precise touch. Sounds like a lot for a hole so short (359 yards from the tips; 336 yards for we mortals) and it is.*

Off the church road, Ballybunion

Some Historical Bits About Ballybunion

The August 19th, 1893, *Limerick Chronicle* included an article about the formation of the Ballybunion Club. It carried the expected details about who was elected to which position — Secretary, Treasurer, President, etc. Then it commented on the twelve holes which comprised the course ("which may be increased should the members so wish"), and a marvelous closing line said, "the course offers every variety of golfing incident."

It is from these "incidents" — the dunes, the streams, the wind — that Ballybunion developed its reputation. But other "incidents" have enhanced that reputation as well.

ooooo

What was known as "the queerest railway in the world" grew out of the efforts of a parish priest from Ballybunion, Father Mortimer O'Connor, and the invention of a monorail by a Frenchman, Charles Francois Marie-Therese Lartique.

The monorail, selected because of its suitability in difficult terrain, ran the whole twelve miles from Listowel to Ballybunion and, appropriately enough, it was called "The Listowel and Ballybunion Railway." When it started operation, Ballybunion had one street, one hotel, a few houses, a post office, and a small police station.

The travel time between the two towns was about forty minutes, and passenger weight had to be evenly distributed on both sides of the "cars."

One of many amusing "incidents" about the railroad reported in Ballybunion's one hundredth anniversary history went as follows: "One lady wanted a piano delivered to Ballybunion, causing consternation in that there was unlikely to be a second (and balancing) piano on the same train. The solution arrived at was to counterbalance with two calves! On the return trip the two calves had to counterbalance each other."

ooooo

As the Ballybunion course developed, modifications to its design took place. Records were not too accurate about who did them, but it is thought that Old Tom Morris of St. Andrews, who was in fact involved with nearby Lahinch in its early years, also contributed to the greatness of Ballybunion. Several others are mentioned over later years, but to what degree would seem to depend on the person telling the story. There is little doubt, however, that Tom Simpson made major contributions to the present-day configuration.

ooooo

It is interesting that women have been "at the heart of the club since foundation." They were invited in the early days to join the Ballybunion Club, just as were men. In 1932, there were 126 men members and 55 women members — hardly an equal balance but a far greater ratio of men to women than most clubs have, even today!

∞∞∞∞

Imagine the 1932 Olympics at Los Angeles being a part of Ballybunion history. It's true. Irishmen Michael Murphy, a steeplechaser, and Eamonn Fitzgerald, who participated in the hop, step, and jump, trained on what is now the fifth fairway.

∞∞∞∞

The 1932 Irish Close Championship for women (pros or amateurs, but they must be Irish) was played at Ballybunion. Five years later, in 1937, Jimmy Bruen won the men's Irish Championship on the old course. He was a mere seventeen years old, and in the finals played the five-time winner, John Burke. To this day, Bruen remains the youngest winner in the event's history. The women's Close was again played at Ballybunion in '58, '71, '79, and '91.

Men's professional events played here include the Irish Professional Championship of 1957, when Harry Bradshaw defeated the other two members of "Irish Golf's Great Triumvirate," Christy O'Connor and Fred Daly, who came in second and third, respectively. As to the quality of those players, Fred Daly was the only Irishman to ever win the British Open, and Bradshaw and O'Connor represented Ireland in the '58 Canada Cup (later to be renamed The World Cup).

The club is rightfully proud of the achievements of Pat Mulcare, who was born and brought up in Ballybunion and learned to play on the Old Course. He played on the Walker Cup team for Britain in 1975 at St. Andrews, where he defeated Dick Siderowf on the eighteenth green of the first day's competition with a fourteen-foot birdie putt. He also contributed to another point on day two with a partnered win over Americans Jerry Pate and Siderowf.

And would you believe that between 1892 and 1993 the club has been captained by no fewer than six reverends?

And on that heavenly note we depart Ballybunion.

TO THE POINT

≈

Jimmy Brosnan is a longtime caddie at Ballybunion. His player, having hit two terrible shots that left him still short of the brook on No. 13 (normally an easy carry on your second shot), asked, "What'll take me across?"

Jimmy responded, first pointing ahead, "There's a bridge right there."

TIRESOME

The eleventh hole at Ballybunion is certainly one of its finest and most difficult. As I prepared to tee off, with the crashing sea immediately off to my right, my caddie said, "Don't be right, sir. All of Ireland is on your left." So warned, I hit my drive into the left rough, and my second shot into the rough, and my third shot into the rough, before finally landing my fourth shot on the green of the par four. As I struggled onto the green, I said "Phew!" in utter exasperation.

To which my caddie responded, "It's a tiring game, sir, when it's badly played."

It's a tiring game.

Wall Alone

Many areas of Ireland are literally peppered with rock formations. Agricultural needs dictated that these rocks be removed, but where to put them? Build stone walls, and that they did. Two interesting facts emerge here; one is that a vast majority of these walls were built by women as their men gathered the stones. The other is that in many cases the walls are signatures of the part of the country they're built in; i.e., this wall is in the north and looks in no way like those in the south, or the west … and so on.

92

COURSE RECORD

I wouldn't say Charlie McCabe was a bad golfer, but one glance at his swing told you he got strokes from most people. So Charlie was more than a little intimidated as the starter on the first tee at Ballybunion. Our caddie told us a little history about the graveyard bordering the right side of the first fairway.

He said the course record for "grave placements" — drives hit into the cemetery — was three, and that the record was held by an inept Scotsman. No sooner said than Charlie launched three drives straight into the graveyard, and not a one of them was ever in doubt.

As we left the tee, the caddie tried to console Charlie by saying, "When back in America, you can tell them you tied a course record at Ballybunion!"

BLESS US, O LORD...

On a gnawing, cold, and drizzly day at Ballybunion some years ago, my foursome was about to tee off at No. 1 when a snugly dressed lady appeared and said she and her friend were in a competition, and being just two of them, would we mind if they went ahead of us. Of course not.

Just as they got out of range and we were again about to tee off, a second pair of ladies approached and said the same. Again we said of course.

When a third pair moved into position for what seemed a further delay, our body language spoke resistance, and one of the little ladies repeated what the first two had said about a competition. Then she demurely added, "You see, we're from a nearby convent and this is our annual event."

Irish boys at play...

For them, golf will come later.

I asked my caddie at
Ballybunion, William
(though pronounced
Willem), how many
children he had.
"Eleven, sir."
"What are their ages?"
"Thirty-something to forty-
something," he replied.

Ireland: The gold at the end of the rainbow.

They seem to exude a gentle love of the game,

Not the winning … or the losing,

Just playing the game …

Whatever the stakes,

Whatever the weather,

Whoever the companions.

Acknowledgments

My editor told me Acknowledgments are read only by those being acknowledged.

That shouldn't be, but he's right. They seem to "toady up" to anyone who's near the author during the book's gestation period; that's wrong. Acknowledgments should be sincere.

They should be as entertaining as the rest of the book (after all, you've paid for the whole book!). So, those acknowledged should come from whoever and whatever has motivated or inspired the author to write the book.

Take Chuck Perry for instance; he's my editor and president of Longstreet. He listened to the idea for the book and said, "Let's go!" We did.

Chuck Perry (far right)

Going back to 1960 . . . "Thanks" to Kevin Durnin, the world's tallest leprechaun. If you catch a leprechaun, they say, he'll show you where the treasure is. I caught Kevin; he showed me the treasure — Ireland. He was general manager for the Irish Tourist Board in North America.

"Six" thanks to Jerry Tarde, Al Barkow, George Peper, Matt Sullivan, Robin McMillan and Mark Brown . . . the scribes who light up the best golf media in America

and who each wrote some ingratiating comments about Ballybunion for my book. And an emphatic thanks to the best golf writer in the world — Herbert Warren Wind — for his wonderful words, probably the first

Ray Ellis

ever done on Ballybunion, in 1971.

Working with Ray Ellis was even better this time than the first. Fortunately, he paints better than he plays golf. His brilliant strokes span the gap from ardent to whimsical, like perhaps no other artist before him.

Then there are the mellow memories of many repeat trips with people like Jim Benham, the ultimate

Doug Cochrane

friend, competitor, golfing partner and gentleman; and our impeccable treasurer Doug Cochrane who keeps a tally on what you won or lost, what you ate and drank and what you owe the pot. There are also the brothers Rex Bob, the official raconteur, on the left and Bill, the senior "Gentle

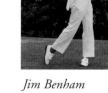

Jim Benham

Bob and Bill Rex

Gordon Dalgleish

Ben" with him.

A big thanks to Gordon Dalgleish, friend first and travel mentor second. No one could do a more considerate job advising us than his golf-travel professionals at PerryGolf have done for many years.

And speaking of travel, we had the kind of cooperation you come to expect of the Irish from Brian

Murphy at Aer Lingus and Orla Carey at the Irish Tourist Board and their staffs.

Other poignant moments I'm grateful for include adventures in some treacherous bunker or berm, that added to my repertoire of golf mess-ups. When these occurred, they seemed damnable but since have given me daunting stories for my home pro and stay-at-home friends.

Ah then…there's that true hero…the Irish pubs and bars. I've almost never seen one I didn't like!

Their lager and stout are wonderful and their blarney may even be better!

Matt and John deGarmo

Finally, thanks to Matthew my son. In addition to being my golfing buddy and a nice guy, he's a sensitive writer who challenges me to write better. If I sound like a proud father, it's because I am.

P.S.

About the people I've left out of the above, it could be fading memory, but, more likely, my editor just said, "Enough!"

Dedication

To RENE, who made me glad I married an Irish girl. She, of the wonderful disposition, for the mothering she has done and still does, for the love that's been constant. I can't believe it — nearly fifty years!

— *John deGarmo*

One of my favorite golf writers, Michael Bamberger, tells the story of an aged Irishman having a lesson on the practice tee. His young teacher says after the lesson, "You're hitting them better today, Mr. McGregor." The old man replies, "I certainly hope so. I'm running out of time."

Those of us who have played this wonderful yet sometimes frustrating game can sympathize with the old gent. Golf is a lifetime experience which reveals so much about one's character. It also prepares one for so many of life's encounters.

I have been fortunate to have played golf for most of my adult life, though not as successfully as I had wanted. I have also painted for most of my life. Fortunately, the latter became my profession and livelihood, so obviously it has been more successful.

My painting career has covered many subjects, but in recent years I have been approached to paint many aspects of golf. Courses throughout the world have offered some of the most beautiful and tranquil landscapes one could imagine. Some of these were depicted in my book *The Spirit of Golf.* The thought never occurred to me that I would be considered a painter of golf. However, I enjoy the reference because I enjoy the game so much, and I dedicate this book to all of my friends with whom I have spent many happy hours on the course.

— *Ray Ellis*

LIST OF PAINTINGS

Paintings are listed consecutively as they appear in book.

Sizes shown are in inches, with vertical measurements first.

Along the Road, 9 $^3/_8$ x 12 $^1/_8$, watercolor

Bucolic, 15 $^1/_2$ x 16 $^1/_2$, watercolor

Vintage Links, 8 x 11 $^1/_2$, watercolor

Nature's Way, 7 $^3/_4$ x 11 $^3/_4$, watercolor

Cap of the Road, 9 x 12 $^1/_4$, watercolor

Irish Troubles, 10 x 14 $^1/_4$, watercolor

#12 at Tralee, 11 $^3/_4$ x 18, watercolor

Shannon Tributary, 12 $^1/_2$ x 18 $^3/_4$, watercolor

Worship on the Ring, 11 $^1/_2$ x 10 $^3/_4$, watercolor

Subtle Three, 13 $^3/_4$ x 21 $^3/_4$, watercolor

Resting Place, 13 x 24 $^1/_2$, watercolor

Megalith, 11 $^3/_4$ x 17 $^1/_2$, watercolor

Gridlock, 8 $^1/_4$ x 12, watercolor

Between the Hills, 12 x 19 $^1/_2$, watercolor

Take the Break Right, 11 $^1/_2$ x 18, watercolor

Stoic, 12 x 18, oil

Rainbow Row, 8 $^3/_4$ x 17 $^1/_2$, watercolor

Promontory, 10 $^1/_4$ x 17 $^1/_2$, watercolor

Soliloquy, 13 $^1/_2$ x 24 $^3/_4$, watercolor

Coming into Town, 11 $^3/_4$ x 17 $^3/_4$, watercolor

Northern Gold, 10 $^3/_4$ x 14, watercolor

Renaissance, 10 $^1/_2$ x 15 $^1/_2$, watercolor

No Relief, 8 x 12, watercolor

The Shrine, 15 $^1/_2$ x 26, watercolor

Down the Chute, 12 x 17 $^3/_4$, watercolor

Long Walk, 12 x 19 $^1/_2$, watercolor

What D'ya Think, 21 $^3/_4$ x 24 $^1/_2$, watercolor

Temptress, 11 x 16, watercolor

Wall Alone, 6 $^3/_4$ x 12 $^1/_4$, watercolor

ABOUT THE AUTHOR

John deGarmo spent twenty-five years as chief executive of his own advertising agency,
where his most gratifying client was Bord Fáilte — The Irish Tourist Board.
DeGarmo has a mid single-digit handicap and at one time served as Advisory
Board Chairman of The American Junior Golf Association. He is also the
creator of The Spirit of Golf.

ABOUT THE ARTIST

Ray Ellis, one of today's most highly regarded impressionist painters, is best known for his best-selling collaborations with Walter Cronkite. He previously collaborated with John deGarmo on The Spirit of Golf.